BEFORE WE FORGET

poems by

Gregg Weatherby

Finishing Line Press
Georgetown, Kentucky

BEFORE WE FORGET

for Joan

*...life is made of ever so many partings
welded together*
—*Charles Dickens*

Copyright © 2022 by Gregg Weatherby
ISBN 978-1-64662-942-8 First Edition
All rights reserved under International and Pan-American Copyright Conventions. No part of this book may be reproduced in any manner whatsoever without written permission from the publisher, except in the case of brief quotations embodied in critical articles and reviews.

ACKNOWLEDGMENTS

Aurora (Online), "Before We Forget" Winner of the Aurora Poetry Prize, "Sunset," Drafts"

Grateful acknowledgement to Frank Murphy, poet, and editor of *Home Planet News Online* for publishing so many of the poems in this collection:

Home Planet News Online #8 "In Loco," "April in Lockdown," "Aloha," "Blue Jay"
Home Planet News Online #7 "Sargasso," "The Old Regulars,"
Home Planet News Online #6 "Red Sky," "Dad's Garden," "Wolf Road"
Home Planet News Online #5 "Short Term," "Subject to Change," "Sweetwater," "May in Iceland"
Home Planet News Online #3 "Ghosts," "Global Warming"
Home Planet News Online #2 (Featured poet w/ Paul Pines) "Dreams"

Also many thanks and acknowledgement to the editors of the following publications for including my work:

Mudfish #22 "Old Friends"
Blueline "Equinox"

Other titles by Gregg Weatherby from Finishing Line Press: *Bone Island; Approaching Home*

Publisher: Leah Huete de Maines
Editor: Christen Kincaid
Cover Art: Caroline Blackburn
Author Photo: Jamie Love
Cover Design: Elizabeth Maines McCleavy and Gregg Weatherby

Order online: www.finishinglinepress.com
also available on amazon.com

Author inquiries and mail orders:
Finishing Line Press
PO Box 1626
Georgetown, Kentucky 40324
USA

Table of Contents

The Old Regulars/McSorley's 1
Drafts 2
Dreams 3
May in Iceland 6
Calculus 7
Ghosts 8
The Ordinary 9
Sargasso 10
Aloha 11
Time Travel 12
Wolf Road and Holy Ground 13
Dad's Garden 14
Fall 16
The Old Farm 17
Sweetwater 18
Equinox 19
Subject to Change 20
Old Friends 21
Still Life with Ghosts 22
April in Lockdown 23
In Loco 24
Silence 25
Red Sky at Morning 26
Buendia Macondo 27
Short Term 28
Haiku 29
Before We Forget 30
Global Warming 31
Blue Jay 32
Notes 33
Sunset 34
Song 35
Birds 36

THE OLD REGULARS/MCSORLEY'S

I don't know why I thought of you
this rainy night
so far removed from the city
and you long gone

I was sitting here quiet upstate
the trees newly leafed suddenly
there were ghosts in the air
                      space and time disappeared
I remembered   when
there were men so sad they didn't know it
the talk the pints
and each man had his own memory
around closing time
when a lone tenor voice
would sing

DRAFTS

What is it
about the sea   what
our need

the rhythm the tides
the salt and softness we float upon
the seeming endlessness of it
all the dark beneath
boiling surf
fascinates
never still yet
it brings a stillness

great blue heron stalks
the shallows high-stepping
at the edge of the park
while over at Scotty's
the boats are in
acres of white canvas
creak of spring lines
of wind in rigging
the ping and ting
like bells
tuned to a different note
the sea breeze savoring the gentle waves
all dreams on deck
drinking the wind

DREAMS

I

Nights I spent dreaming
of horses and riding
Sunny the grumpy palomino
Mr. T and Bootjack both spooked unlucky bays
Dream Catcher the goofy App mare
all gone now
eight hours in the saddle and open country
stiff old chaps friendly
rain shaped hat
good weather, bad
doesn't matter the old cowboy says
nothing you can do but enjoy it
the squeak of smooth saddle like an old chair
smell of leather sweet hay and horses
how quiet I was then
alone
and not much talk from the animals
only on Christmas eve
Mo used to say before she died

except for the ranch owners
best job I ever had

found my snaffle and bridle
green in a bag on a shelf
my old saddle
somewhere
lost

how often I dream
of horses

II

There's a dream
where I can't move
wedged in the corner of the wheelhouse
heavy seas
foul weather gear
survival suited
then calm open water
on deck in the sun
making good time
logging hours at the wheel
if the captain's willing

nights rigging the spring lines
drinking beer still swaying on my feet
diesel smell of the engine room so clean you could
painting the hull suspended
in a bosun's chair
changing the zinc
the captain splicing lines
or showoff knots
one foot on the wheel
just for the hell of it

the low pay didn't bother me then
the SRO don't call it a hotel
where I stayed that year
the Mexicans one senorita I remember
but that's another story
wouldn't stay there again
it's gone now
liked that job but
almost winter winds

straight northerly frigid channel
pulling navaids
chipping ice off the deck
never be warm again
I thought

how often I dream of the sea

MAY IN ICELAND

I don't know about September

what I thought
at the edge of the falls
hearing the last syllable the echo
of crashing glacier water
mixing with the sound of rain
huddled in my heavy clothes
for the long walk back

in May at the old place of the law
the place of truth
is a lonely place to stand
a rock overlooking
a rift in the earth
weeks before I begin my treatment

looking up the valley
the fault is
a long zipper-like scar
the boundaries of stark black basalt
pulling apart sinking slowly
some day the icy sea

CALCULUS

Fall is the season of remembering
the leaves last flame to dying
dry and brittle as old hearts
it takes an act of will to recall what
had been before our attempts to warm
against the coming cold
truth in fragments
change over change

I keep coming back
(they keep poisoning me
I keep coming back)
returning
like the next dream
no thought of time
but time enough
I suppose
change in me
over change in you

we are what we leave behind

an old fedora
a knit tie
photos of forgotten people
notes about birthdays

small things
that make clearer
a life whole
the trajectory of lines
never quite complete

GHOSTS

September the leaves already float
against the window like ghosts

bringing dreams
of places you never intended
where time is kept by bells
some forgotten or broken items
disappear into thin night
a glass set on a table
a teacup in a saucer

windchimes in dead calm
the old floorboards creak and pop
whine of old timbers
a sigh through the walls
any of these sounds might move
the house marks a passage

images frail and fragile
sometimes a breeze brings
a slight scent of age
of clear blue sky
when the windows shudder

I pull the blanket over my head
like a cowl
let the cold wind pass by

it's all about the dark

sometimes I stay up all night
waiting

THE ORDINARY

The new moon suspended
across the darkening
high-pressure sky
another passing phase they say
surviving is what we do

I pass the cemetery
without stopping
the hospital without stopping
the church without stopping
the places
where silence is ordinary
surviving is what we do

not noticing
the circularity of lives
the passing of people
without stopping
surviving is what we do
where silence is ordinary
the ordinary is what we do

SARGASSO

I wait for the mailman every day

regretfully
the cards and letters
do not keep pouring in
thank you

sorry
we are not all
in one place
and I am too busy writing things like this
to look up old addresses
even though
I'd love to tell you
how the sweeping palm
in the front yard
brushes the awning in soft breezes
or about the cactus
that flowers every evening
about long days on the beaches
nights alone in bars

ALOHA

I was coming back from Japan
and I remember in Hawaii
in an old rundown dive bar a place
only the locals would dare go
I thought I saw him in a dark corner
a silent shadow alone in sunlight and dust
even when I said hi as I left no words
but he was on Broadway then
and later after I had run
away from the city and I was in my
condemned trailer on the mountain
huddled in the cold corner wind
through the floorboards snow
on the sills staring at nothing
nothing at all and my friends said
you must come but I couldn't go
couldn't go couldn't explain how I was
a prisoner of the dark
I thought they wouldn't understand
much later Lisa told me he died
of a stroke all alone a shadow
in sunlight and dust
no words at all

TIME TRAVEL

The particulars of any random day
the wind off the water the quality
of light a certain time and place
a song a scent a wrong turn
the clocks revolve past all windows

or how someone's name
stops you in your tracks
a sudden strange dance of time
and breath

or if you sit all afternoon
on a rocky cliff
overlooking a mountain lake

WOLF ROAD AND HOLY GROUND

It's a steep hill a slow climb a dirt track
on the north edge of the cemetery
Wolf Road where we went as teenagers
much as we could
to neck and drink beer watch the stars move
no thought for the sleeping dead

the radio and the sound of our breaths
our world was wild
blackberries in brambles and sumac
the dark was deeper than the trees

the moon and headlights pushed shadows
of trees in slow motion
the cemetery to the left just as steep
as the road the family plot
first grandma then mom and dad
near the top the cornfields

begin there and hay fields I think back so long
when I was a teenager every time I'm there
the startle and thought the strange juxtaposition
of holy ground and Wolf Road
I visited more often then

now through the long stretch
of lost time of missed visits
the only sound on the hill
my own

DAD'S GARDEN

The garden was beyond
the last row of pine
maybe half a basketball court of sloping land
flooded in the spring
even before Mom put out the mums
and herb pots or planted her flowers
along the verge of the house
he'd call our neighbor
old Mr. Barrows
to come with his wheezing yellow Chalmers
to plow and disc
every year we'd pick the rocks that grew there

though we all worked it
everyone knew it was Dad's garden
it was his on his hands and knees
all summer after work
singing softly a song
I don't remember or
making small unintelligible noises
as he went pulling weeds
tossing rocks

I remember what Dad said
about gardening
even now

plant garlic by the full moon
nearest Columbus Day
harvest in spring
after the first green
shoots of horseradish appear above the snow

hang the garlic
in onion bags from the cellar rafters
dark and cool
plant nothing else until
after Memorial Day

then
asparagus comes first
pick it before it flowers

tomatoes in the thick of summer
and sweet corn
both so plentiful people would
give them away
hang them in bags
on your door

then the kitchen would be busy
mom canning and freezing
making ketchup sauce and what she called chili
somehow this fall activity is
mixed with springtime
when dad would pull the horseradish
grind and prepare it

hot and bitter
as tears

FALL

The end of all this autumn
the end of all this
the end of autumn is never quiet
storm/wind
swirling color of leaves
all gone
the next day

THE OLD FARM

Collecting sad footsteps in the field
maybe a fortune in forgotten dusty carriages
in the old barn mice in the seat cushions
cobwebs stalls dry as dust
floating in streams of alternating sun
and shadow gray fences
undone horses all gone buried out back
I knew all their names

unmarked quarter-mile track
grown to weeds harness and tack
so brittle it breaks in your hand
only the willow is green and bends
there is no one here I knew
their names and all at once
we are gone or we are no longer young
the meaning of morning of sunsets
shifts it is autumn and I wait for that
day at sunrise the leave's colors
pop full out suddenly wind and rain
the trees are bare
and we long for Spring

I ought to keep doing something
else but I've forgotten why
did I stop here where
did a whole day go why
is there always dark but
sometimes there is light

SWEETWATER

When the days warm
but the nights were still cold
we'd go to the sugarbush
in the hollow down the hill
and run the metal buckets back
through the snow and mud
dump them in the seemingly towering tank
on top of the heavy wooden sled
pulled by Ike and Bessie the old draft horses
icy water filling our boots sodden
mittens sagging
we didn't mind
later as the day's light changed
we'd warm up in the sap house
smells of sweet steam and wood fire
boiling hot dogs
in one of the rows of evaporating pans
eating the thick syrup on the snow
a lifetime ago it seems
when there was white smoke
in the dark gray woods each spring
and the mark of heavy horseshoes
in the undisturbed snow
the unused dirt road

EQUINOX

First day of spring
means nothing here
the earth starts its tilt
towards the sun
lake effect
flakes fly from the northwest
the late-night silence of snow offers
three to five inches
of no accumulation
the sky gray
for days

and the light
       (what there is of it
throws its blanket
over potential brilliance
of snow
fog is the angels' share
and the willow dips its fingers
into the stream

no
significant sun
for days now the
windows rattle in their frames
whether we like it or not
the earth bows to spring
in its own good time

SUBJECT TO CHANGE

The icy footprints marking the yard
grow large and disappear
mounds of snow shrink in cold rain
what is left behind lingers
the things we keep coming back to
St. Francis emerges
with the first green on the lawn
March evening's wet snow gone
by afternoon as breezes shift south
maple sap rises
pushing gray branches into life
morning phoebe returns
the sun heads north
we turn the clocks ahead
and come full circle

OLD FRIENDS

Not everyone knows the quiet
on the porch the sun the soft breeze
the talk of what we were
back then and no longer
but sometimes as clear
as yesterday was sometimes
not so clear and some remembered
quite differently as we tried
to identify birds in flight
or by their song

we could watch the accumulating
clouds and years go by and catch
the smell of hay from the barn
the old Ford tractor in the field
where two young boys fit and trim
bucked hay without tiring
in the summer sun
all day and hay dust and sweat
almost sixty years ago
and my friend remembers his dad
coming apart bit by bit
hay still in the barn the cows
sold at auction before he died
saying "take me to the junkyard"
and we stared silently
across the field

STILL LIFE WITH GHOSTS

Two months into lockdown
at a certain hour of night
time stops cold sneaks in
under the doors through the windows
the ghosts you are left with
come in dreams softly elusive
lost sometimes you wonder
about pictures from long ago places
and people you used to know
what have they found where
did they go alone in the quiet night
the ringing in your ears

APRIL IN LOCKDOWN

Late on a cold and windy afternoon
snow still in the air trees
bare the time of the plague
after a long day at work staring
at the computer a month on
under lockdown the new sensations
face masks and enforced seclusion
I understand now the songs my father sang
only to himself under his breath
why he was afraid of the cold
felt the chill all year long
why he stopped going to memorials
my age moves across me like
the edge of dark on the Earth
from space you can't tell
what we have done the destruction
the species disappearing before I knew
they were even here
the tired senselessness of it all
the coming dark the silent cold
massive moon lights the empty yard
I forgot why I was singing
"happy birthday" two times

IN LOCO

There are worse places
to be inside any of my old apartments
in the city the only views smudged
sooty windows pigeon-filled
airshafts and garbage-strewn
back alleys heavy metal gates for shutters
no sun ever

here there is light and glass due east
due west views of round red maple
willow shagbark rising sun
and setting sun and birds
oh the birds I know some of them
by name now one female cardinal
at the feeder three times a day her mate
posing in the tree mourning doves
three species of woodpeckers
elegant in their black-and-whites
and little wrens

on the news the curve resists flattening
who would have thought in the city
reefer trucks are used for bodies
no sound in the streets
in the Spring rain in the burning bush
shelter in place

SILENCE

Here in this time when every day
is the same and the same
birds come to the feeder and the same
nothing but ourselves
such quiet wanders the house
a long ellipsis of sadness
dreaming of islands and different light
and my hair gets longer and
I feel older than I did before
I wish it were Spring on the deck
but it's April and still snow and cold
and the time of the plague
and the annoyances of solitude
magnify the silence
the silence of it all

RED SKY AT MORNING

Weeks of red eye
of sunset
the Everglades on fire hell
the whole state on fire
        and half of Georgia too

red sun mornings greet the early arrivals
        a month too soon
the rainy season
and the first named storm
slams at the metal roof
keeps me from exhausted sleep

this fog this end of days haze
this acrid taste of air
and the aquifer
bone dry
welcomes the saline sea

time
and what remains
the haunting
burning eyes

of red sunsets red dawns
we have made
hell
from now on
will bear our name

BUENDIA MACONDO

One mile down and ninety days
thick sweet crude rushed into the sea
deep water clouded gas volatile
aromatics and the thick air
flows off the gulf
breezes cool the shimmering heat
waves wash tar
along the white sand beaches
red muck on the tides the sea grass
the coastal marshes

we believe stiffly in the wind
yet turn our backs to it

oil soaked seagull pecks at the slick-
stained hull of a cleanup boat
brown pelican coasts
into the onshore breeze

SHORT TERM

Maybe the problem is
we spend too much of our time
looking down at our feet or anyway
maybe just a little
ahead not far enough look
where it gets us
generations saddled with debt super bugs
bad food bad air ozone
oil slicks into the seas' beaches the Gulf
tarred and feathered running
out of time and down hill
will we disappear
like the fleeting ghost of a dream
a jar of ashes
tossed in the wind

HAIKU

1.

Springtime in New York,
Sitting with haiku masters,
No pen, no paper

2.

If you sit quiet
On the porch writing poems
All manner of birds

3.

Not easy to eat,
My voice like wind through bamboo.
No wine; much sadness.

BEFORE WE FORGET

Driving after three months in lockdown
along a familiar route it seems
there used to be more trees
where did they go where
is the shade the summer breeze
how can there be bare branches
lit up with yellow finches
out my window in the afternoon
winter sun when there aren't any
trees I mean why can't we leave them
alone when will they blossom and leaf
this Spring while we are locked down
doing less with less stuck at home
during the quarantine trees have disappeared
from familiar roadsides
I realize I am no longer young

If there are no trees where
will the blue jay call in his complaints
what about the red and grey squirrels
or me on the balcony today transfixed
by the cardinal's red the trees
breathing branches lifting falling
in rhythm to my own

GLOBAL WARMING

Ten straight days
no sun and cold so cold
it radiates off coats even inside
we huddle against it
seems winter gets colder every year
another ice age cometh maybe
just old age creeping in
through the cracks summers hotter
too the next great extinction man
oh man

still the deserts push into verdancy
ice caps melt northwest
passage free and clear
glaciers disappear islands
sink in rising seas our lives
thin blood cools so

the hour grows late
bank the fire try to find
some comfort some grace

BLUE JAY

Woodpeckers eat fashionably late
at the feeder
the last of the oak leaves drift
down circling in slow motion

a blue jay lands on the railing
and calls out
we regard each other

it is November the first snow
and 25% of his species is gone
maybe forever the snow mixes with rain
falls on his lost habitat
we regard each other
in silence

NOTES

No sign all summer
of cardinal or little wren even

the leaves wave quietly
the tv silenced
the politics of madness

the sudden return of birds
signals a change of seasons

on the table a book of poems
a book about birds
a magazine article says
one-third are lost

there are notes that we cannot hear
there are notes that we cannot sing

SUNSET

Just after the summer solstice
in the shallow water of twilight
near silence in the steady rain
no birds even

my gaze is pulled by the waves
to islands
there is a different gravity
off the mainland

time is quiet
insistent dreams of ghosts
old addresses haunt me
even in daylight a sense
that it's time
a bubble effervescent
evanescent
floating to its ending
to the taut surface
of its ending

SONG

The sunrise begins
to peek at the day
each tree dances in the wind
in its own way
summer finally arrived

you leave one place
to find another
handful of memories
while we have them
fading into the darkness of legacy

finches sing in the dense wood you know
not where the song goes not where it ends

BIRDS

Not long in the future
standing among what's left
of the trees
a young child will ask
were there birds do you remember
the birds what were they like
what language did they speak
what were their names
is this their place
where did they go
what did you do

www.ingramcontent.com/pod-product-compliance
Lightning Source LLC
LaVergne TN
LVHW041552070426
835507LV00011B/1051